Growth and Development *of* Ranikhet Township in Twentieth Century

Kamna Lohani

ANAMIKA PUBLISHERS & DISTRIBUTORS (P) LTD.
4697/3, 21A, Ansari Road, Daryaganj, New Delhi 110002
Phones: 011-2328 1655, 011-43708938
E-mail: anamikapublishers@yahoo.co.in

First Published 2021

ISBN 978-81-7975-700-0

PRINTED IN INDIA

Published by Anamika Publishers & Distributors (P) Ltd., 4697/3, 21A, Ansari Road, Daryaganj, New Delhi 110002. Typeset by Shivani Compuers, Delhi 110093 and Printed at Vikas Computer & Printers, Tronica City, Ghaziabad

Contents

Acknowledgements

The author takes this opportunity to express her deep sense of reverence, admiration and gratitude to Prof. Shekhar Pathak (Historian) for his motivation to write about Ranikhet, to Prof. Anil Joshi for his valuable guidance, useful suggestions and untiring assistance in the preparation of the manuscript.

She is highly grateful for the unqualified cooperation and consideration extended to her by executive officer and staff of Cantonment Board Ranikhet.

She is equally gratefull to Prof. V.N Dinesh for his motivation to get this work done. Last but not least author is highly overwheled by time to time emotional support rendered by her parents Late Shri A.D. Joshi (Father) Mrs. Keshvi Joshi (Mother), Sri U.C. Joshi (Brother), Sri Dinesh Chandra Lohani (Husband) and Chinmaya and Kartikey her sons, without which this work could not have taken off.

Place : Dehradun **Dr. Kamna Lohani**

Authors Pen

I was born and brought up in Ranikhet. Naturally there remained a desire in my heart to write about the place where I spent my first sixteen years and to which I have an enduring attachment.

As the years progressed, my desire to bering a quill to my town became stronger still. When I became a student of History, this longing urged me into an attempt to write about the origin and fate of this sleepy town through a Historical lens. This text in the product of my endeavour to chart the contemporary history and development of Ranikhet.

In terms of its timeline this book Covers the period of Ranikhet's history from the early 1900 almost to the end of 20th century. The primary motivation to earmark this particular period was that it (quite narrowly) escapes the digital age. While one cannot access the events of this time as easily as one would for more recent years. I want this book to be able to bring the beautiful and simple Ranikhet from a few decades ago into the reader's lap.

I delved into chronicles of the Cantonment Board of Ranikhet to guide this book. I reinforced the narratives with documents of Uttar Pradesh government, interviews with elders and with some minor help from my own recollections. I am hopeful that this text will not only shed some light on the history of the large city of Ranikhet and Kumaon regiment but also visit the quirks of the old hamlet of Ranikhet.

Finally I want to dedicate this book to my beloved parents under whose watchful gaze I grew to adore this city. I hope this can be a small token of my love for them and for those idyllic times.

Kamna Lohani

A VIEW OF HIMALAYA

"I wish more of our people living in plains below would visit the Himalayas....They can have their fill of flowers there and noble trees and primeval forests. They can breathe the free unstained air which invigorates and they can return strengthened in body and mind and spirit."

Pandit Jawahar Lal Nehru

1

Introduction

Kumaon — A Brief History

It is safe to assume that during the dark ages the region now known as Kumaon consisted of a number of petty principalities. It consolidated after centuries of warfare into one state under the "CHAND RAJAS".

The founder of the CHAND dynasty was Som Chand, a Chandra Vanshi Rajput. He came from the plains as an adventurer, married the Raja of Sira's daughter and later supplanted his Father-in-Law. The date of his accession may be taken as 953 AD. In its early significance Kumaon denotes the tract of country lying along the right bank of the river Kali and it is not till after the CHANDS had their capital shifted to Almora in 1563 A.D. That the name of Kumaon covered the present limits of Pitthoragarh, Almora and Nainital Districts. The commencement of the decline of the Chand power may be dated from the reign of Devi Chand (1720 - 26). Internal troubles and quarrels arose to such an extent that the Gurkhas when they crossed the Kali river in

1790 A.D., had a very easy task in conquering the region. Having conquered and occupied Kumaon, the Gurkhas gradually extended their conquest over Garhwal and the Dun Valley.

Aggression by the Gurkhas upon the British territory determined Lord Hastings to declare war in 1814 A.D.. In January 1815 A.D a column of 3,000 men under Lt. Colonel Kosi Gardener advanced upto river Kosi to attack Almora, while Captain Hearsey with 1500 men entered the river Kali. The column under Colonel Gardener was more successful and after driving out Gurkhas from amongst other places - Kumpur where they had entered themselves, arrived on 27th March at Katarmal, 7 miles from Almora. After a decisive battle at Sitoli on the outskirts of Almora the Gurkhas were literally ousted and by the treaty of Sitoli in 1815, the whole of Kumaon passed under the British regime.

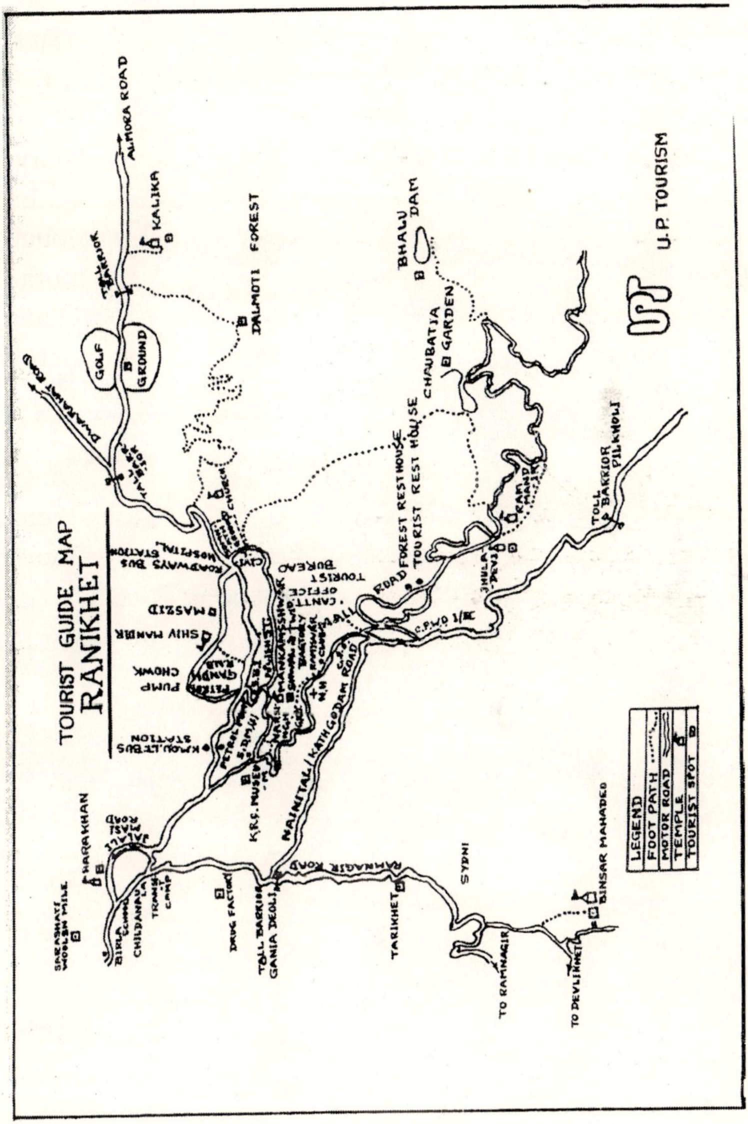
TOURIST GUIDE MAP
RANIKHET
ALMORA ROAD
KALIKA
DALMOTI FOREST
BHALU DAM
CHAUBATIA GARDEN
GOLF GROUND
FOREST REST HOUSE
TOURIST REST HOUSE
ROADWAYS BUS STATION
TOURIST BUREAU
MASZID
SHIV MANDIR
CHURCH
NAINITAL / KATHGODAM ROAD
RAMNAGAR ROAD
K.R.S. MUSEUM
DRUG FACTORY
TOLL BARRIOR
GANIA DEOLI
TARIKHET
SYDNI
BINSAR MAHADEO
TO RAMNAGIR
TO DEVLIKHET
TOLL BAKRIOR PILKHOLI
U.P. TOURISM
LEGEND
FOOT PATH
MOTOR ROAD
TEMPLE
TOURIST SPOT

2

The Queen of Kumaon Hills - Ranikhet

Ranikhet, the very name conjures up a vivid image - a sleepy little town, scintillatingly, beautiful, thickly wooded, verdent, fresh and endowed with every thing that nature could bestow. Its innumerable bungalows with their exotic nomenclature leads one to wonder, whether this is an Indian town or an extension of the Scottish Highlands.

One of the finest hill stations in the world, Ranikhet is situated in the Almora District of the state of Uttarakhand. For those, who go to the hills for rest and relief from the fiery summer of the plains and the din and dust and the bustle of big cities, Ranikhet is an ideal place for holidaying with its good roads, open spaces, places for mountaineering, hiking, Qolfing, shooting and angling.

Yet it is quite astonishing to discover that till the third quarter of the last century few people had even heard of this place. The purpose of this study is to trace the birth and development of the jewel of a town known as Ranikhet.

Kumaon's glacial valleys and mountain peaks have

hypnotized travellers since time immemorial. Distinct from the rest of the Himalayas, Kumaon still retains the relics of the pre British era. To the holidayers, Ranikhet offers the blue-green panoramic view and sunny days of laughter and fun.

Justice William O Douglas of the U.S. Supreme Court had said "Ranikhet is easily the finest hill station in the World".

Ever if this be far too a sweeping conclusion, it won't be inappropriate to describe Ranikhet as the idyllic hamlet of Kumaon. As the majestic Himalayas rise tall and mighty against the still blue sky. Ranikhet lies snugly pursed on a ridge, thickly wooded with Pine, Deodar and Oak trees.

It's salubrous climate and congenial atmosphere has made Ranikhet one of the most sort after hill resorts of the country. Circled by streams, varied ecological riches and undulating mountain ranges, Ranikhet is one of those very few towns of the country which are still very close to nature and have somehow managed to suffer pretty little from the ravages of present day exploitation.

Speaking strictly in terms of topography, Ranikhet is cordoned off by the Tibet in the far North, Nainital District on the South, by Garhwal on the West and by the Kingdom of Nepal on the far East. It lies entirely within the Himalayan system. However, the great snow mountains which form such a conspicuous feature of the view from Ranikhet do not lie along the ridge. Most of them are situated at the Southern extremity of snow clad spurs standing South of the ridge and at the distance of 30 to 50 Kms. The altitude of Ranikhet is 1829 Metres.

All the main forests are situated in the immediate neighbourhood of Ranikhet, Chaubattia and Lalkurti Bazar.

Only one small block detached forest is however situated at Upat about 3 miles from Ranikhet on the Almora Motor Road. The Cantonment forests are bound practically on all the sides by the forests of Ranikhet range of West Almora Division.

3

Topography of Ranikhet

The Cantonment comprising the Ranikhet proper, Kumpur, Chaubattia and Dulikhet is about 6 Kms long with an average breadth of 3 Kms and has an area of 4083 acres.

There is also an outlying portion called Upat some 3 Kms away on the Almora road where the Golf links are located.

The station lies high being 5,966 Kms feet at the standing came 5,983 feet at pinnacle hill (Kumpur) and 6,942 feet at Chaubattia.

Ranikhet topographically is surrounded by the Tibet in the Far North, Nainital district on the South, by Garhwal on the West and by the Kingdom of Nepal on the Far East. It lies within the Himalayan system.

Standing at an altitude of 1829 metres Ranikhet presents to its viewers the snow clad mountain, the lush green forests and a scenic beauty comparable to that of the Scottish Highlands.

It is well intersected with good roads and has great advantages in the matter of level ground and the possibilities of expansion.

The slopes and ravines in the Cantonment are well wooded and the sale of firewood forms an important part of the income of Cantonment fund. The trees are principally the Chir - Pine, Janj-Oak and Rhododendron. The willow and alder are also common in damp situations. The Deodars, Chestnuts and horse Chestnuts are not indigenous to Ranikhet.

Natural Beauty

Ranikhet is surrounded by the forests of Pine and Oak. Its evergreen vistas of exquisite beauty and the sapphire of encircling hills blend with deep blue cloudless skies. They have a charm of their Himalayan peaks glistening in the distance.

Venues of Pine, Deodar and the cypress trees line the road side along with an occasional sprinkling of Oak and Rhodendron.

Ranikhet commands a remarkable view of the central Himalayan range extending from the peaks of Api and Nampa in Western Nepal to the snows of Sri Badrinath and Tehri Garhwal in the West. These snow clad mountains stretch across a length of about 120 miles. In the clear morning atmosphere these lofty pinnacles of unstained, snow appear before the eyes in a gigantic sweep.

The following peaks can be seen from Ranikhet from West to East:-

Bandarpanch	20,731 Feet
Jaunli	21784 "
Bartakhanta	21594 "
Kharchkund	21785 "
Badrinath	22395 "

Kimatung	21226	"
Nalikhanta	21713	"
Tibet Border	25443	"
Mana	23862	"
Rataban	22141	"
Trishul	23406	"
Dunagiri	23184	"
East Trishul	22360	"
Nandadevi	25660	"
Nandakot	22530	"
Pancha Chuli	22661	"
Tilkot	22114	"
Nampa	23352	"

NATURAL CONDITIONS

1. Soil

The soil of Ranikhet is a light sandy loam derived mostly from mica schists and gneiss. In moist ravines and hollows and in places above the altitude limit of Chir, there is good mould layer making the soil well suited to the growth of Oak and broad leaved species, on some of the ridges and southerly aspects in the Chir zones, especially where grazing has been heavy in the past. The soil is proper being shallow and dry, but on the whole soil is good and has greatly improved since the forests have been adequately protected.

2. Climate

As might be expected in an area with an average altitude of 6,000 feet the climate is good and salubrious. It is cold during winter. Snowfall occurs in most of the years and in the years of heavy snowfall it stays in sheltered places even for about a month. Frost is common but is not severe.

Light winter rains usually occur in the latter half of December, January and February during which period snow falls in higher levels but does not persist for long on the ground. Thunder storms some times occur in May and June. Summer monsoon rains usually begin towards the end of June and last until the end of September. Severe winds are infrequent.

3. Temperature In Summer

Maximum 32.2 C
Mimimum 8.4 C

4. Temperature In Winter

Maximum 7.2 C
Minimum 3.3 C

5. Rainfall

127 cm (50 inches average)

6. Altitude

1829 metres

7. Clothing Required

Summer - Light woolen or cotton.
Winter - Heavy woolen.

8. Population

As per census figure of 1981 it was 18,190.

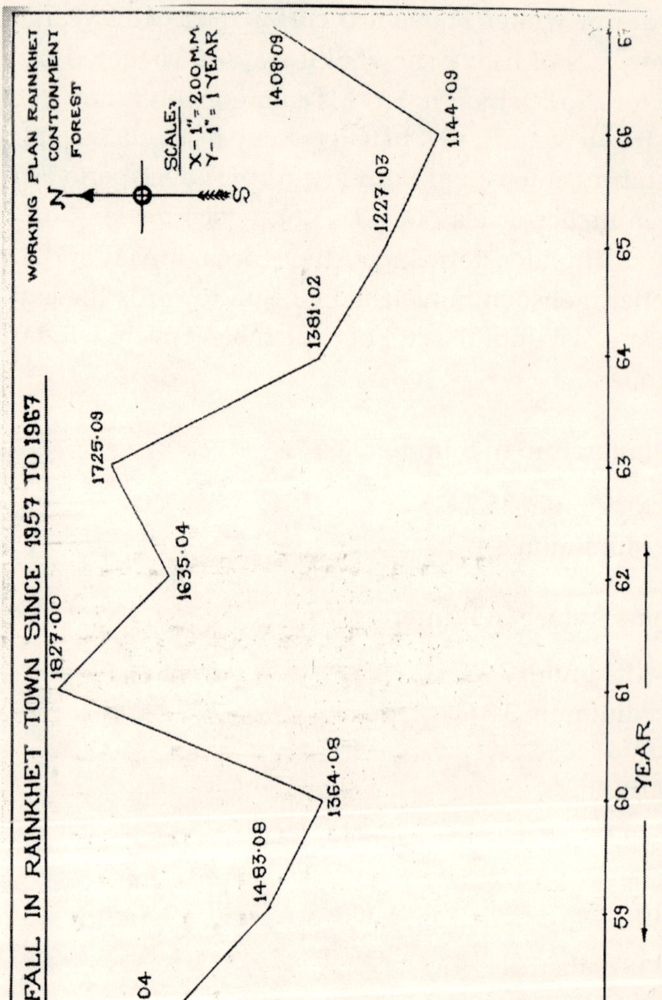
ANNUAL RAINFALL IN RAINKHET TOWN SINCE 1957 TO 1967
WORKING PLAN RAINKHET
CONTONMENT
FOREST
N
S
SCALE,
X – 1" = 200 M.M.
Y – 1" = 1 YEAR
1262·06
1697·04
1483·08
1364·08
1827·00
1635·04
1725·09
1381·02
1227·03
1144·09
1408·09
X
1800
1600
1400
1200
1000
0
1957
58
59
60
61
62
63
64
65
66
67
YEAR
M.M.

4

Antiquity

ORIGIN OF THE WORD RANIKHET

Ranikhet literally means the "Queen's field" and the legend is that a Queen by the name of Padmini, wife of King Sudhar Dev 1180 A.D. encamped here and somewhere down near the present site of the settled Ranikhet Club, and gave the name to the locality. Whatever may the origin of the legend be, the hill station of Ranikhet has justified its name.

The other hearsay is that Ranikhet was the scene of many battles and that the name is a corruption of the words "Ran-Kshetra" meaning the field of battle.

No trace of the place of king Sudhardev can be found today, but the place remained the same bewitching, full of flower's trees and green meadows in he midst of heavenly Himalayan surroundings. Lost into oblivion for long, the picturesque hill elation was rediscovered by the Britishers. This is said that they bought it from the local villagers to build it as a summer resort and establish an army recruitment centre. Ranikhet had everything to soothe the nerves of avid city dwellers as were British, the salubrious atmosphere, tall conifer trees, green meadows, serene surroundings absolute peace and the hospitable people the charm of every season was irresistible in its own way that made Ranikhet a destination for the British.

5

Development of Ranikhet Under British Rule

Once Kumaon had been conquered by British, various Europeans subsequently acquired land in Almora district and among them the troup family, Colonel R. Troup of 63rd N.I. and his sons Captain R.H.W. Troup of 35th Royal Troop, Captain C.T.R. Troup of 52nd Oxford light infantry and Mr. N. Troup purchased from the villagers - Chaubattia, which was named Oakland, Holm Farm, Kumpur, Ranikhet and Upat and started tea plantation.

In 1868 Sir William Mansfield the then Commander-in-Chief sent Sergeant Major Lang of the 23rd Royal Welsh Fusilers to look for sites in hill stations for British troops. Ranikhet having been selected as the most suitable, the estate of the Troup family were acquired by the Government and the Cantonment came into existence in 1869 A.D.

In 1870 Log Huts were put up for accomodating the troops which arrived in the form of First Royal Scots and detachment of 37th Hampshire Regiment. They were entrusted with a job of making roads as well as clearing and levelling of the sites where barracks would be constructed.

Earlier a detachment of 25th Kings Own Scottish Borderers were sent to Seoni which was also viewed as a perspective Cantonment, but subsequently this idea fizzled out.

Lord Mayo the then Governor General happened to spend some days at Ranikhet and was so taken with Chaubattia that he had a survey made for a railway line from Ramnagar to Ranikhet. The scheme was pronounced quite feasible and had Lord Mayo lived long enough, the summer seat of the Government of India would have been transferred from Simla to Ranikhet.

The oldest house built by the British was a dak bungalow which is now the residence of the Sub-Divisional Officer. The Officer's mess at Chaubattia was originally named Glenronnock and was a property of the Troup family as also was the Holm Farm and Holm Cottage. ,

The first shop to deal in European goods was that of Messrs. Rustomjee and Sons, who had migrated to this area in 1876. With the setting up of the Cantonment Board, there was a sudden influx of people who came down and settled in Ranikhet, namely the merchant entraders, army contractors, retired civil servants and people following different vocations.

Another interesting aspect connected with the development of the town is the fact that it was conceived *as* an ideal place where all the lady wives of the British army Officers serving in any part of the country could be housed. Hence the construction of innumerable bungalows, scattered all over the landscape, all connected with proper roads and provided with every possible facility available at that time.

The number of these lady wives' was so large that Ranikhet was often referred to as BIBIANA (meaning the board of wives). Since all the families were residing at

Ranikhet it was but natural that the entire mail coming from their home (England) was first brought to Ranikhet where it was sorted and thereafter distributed all over the country. As such, the Ranikhet Post Office was called the General Post Office (a name it continuous to enjoy to this day despite the fact that it is not a GPO today). The Post Master resided at a beautiful bungalow just opposite to the Post Office known as the Hermitage.

It has been the tradition that all the serving and retired army personnel who were enamoured of the place, selected their favourite sites, which reminded them of their native place and not only built bungalows there, but also gave them the same name which was of their home in England. They led a very luxurious and a stately life, such as having their own barbers, washerman and a motley of attendants.

At that time the Kumaon Commissionary had 3 districts-Almora, Nainital and Garhwal,and the Ranikhet treasury was the head treasury of Almora and some areas of Garhwal too. The old pensioners used to bring ghee from Garhwal in exchange for salt.

The Somnath ground was then called Dulikhet. It is said, its contractor, Chamu Khan suffered a loss. On Wednesdays and Saturdays it turned out to be a race course for not only horses but for dogs too. On Fridays, Mission School students used to play, games there, during the day.

The Nar Singh ground was called the Alma ground. Lalkurti bazar was also known as B.I. (British Infantry) *bazar of* the Kumpur. Though there was a Sadar bazar in every Cantonment, the Mall was also found in other cities but the Zaroori bazar (meaning the necessary market) was only in Ranikhet. There was also a red light area known as the Troup Ganj. A portion of the Sadar bazar which was built by

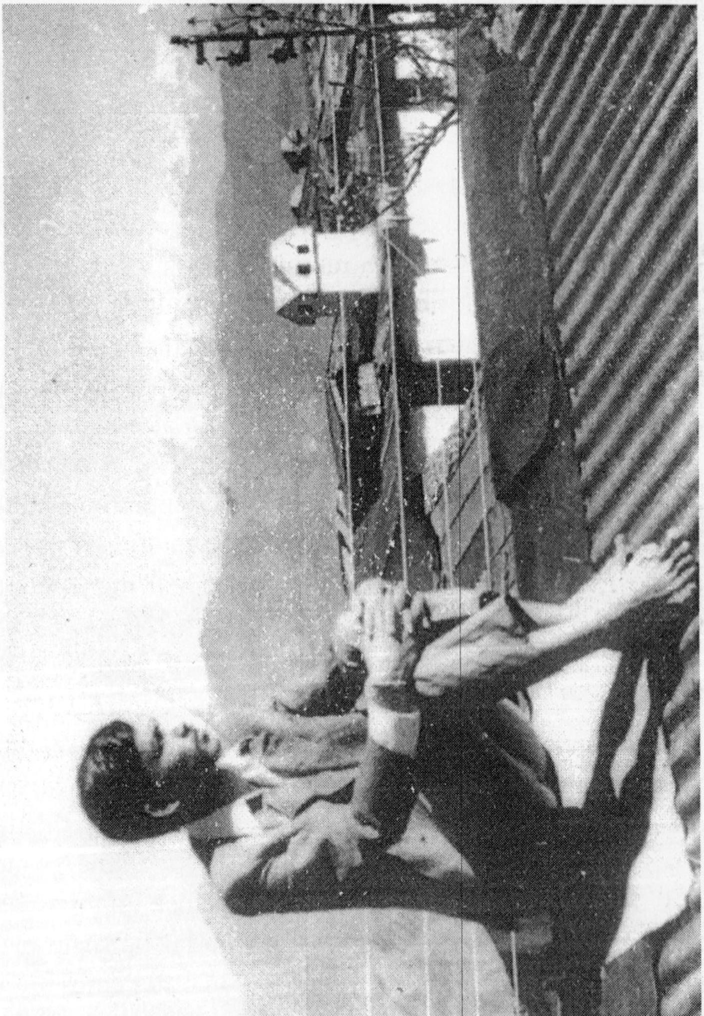

Captain R.H.W. Troup known as the Troup Ganj was still in the possession of the family of Troup, which was later on sold to one of the most prestigious lawyer of Ranikhet - Sir Sridher Joshi. It is now, known as, Sridher Ganj.

6

The Development of Town

TRADE, COMMERCE AND TERTIARY SERVICES

The establishment of the Cantonment at Ranikhet lured many merchants and traders who flocked in numbers excited as they were at the prospect of good business. The Sadar bazar developed into a cosmopolitan market place with the English, Anglo Indians, Chinese, Parsis, Muslims,Kashmiris and Marwaris, rubbing shoulders against one another in their crest for making the fast buck. The suddenness of this take over of the market by the more sophisticated outsiders overawed and pulverized the local traders, mostly Brahmins and Shahs, who had to rest content with selling their wares in the not so glamorous Khari and Zaroori bazar (Necessary Market).

An important factor behind the development of Ranikhet as a major trading centre was that apart from being a Cantonment, it was also the farthest place in entire Kumaon, which could be reached by a proper motor road.

From here, all the other places were accessible only by horses and mules. Hence, it was only obvious that Ranikhet became a haven for wholesellers, commission agents, transporters etc. etc.

The Sadar bazar was dotted with a number of Coffee Shops, billiard saloons, and bars. Needless to say that these were accessible only to the white skinned and the affluent natives. Gradually some auxiliary shops also came into being, viz; Latif Motor Garaze-1931, a petrol shop (petrol was at that time sold in Cans, there was no petrol pump). The shopping centres of the British time continue to exist even today although the ownership and the nature of trade has undergone a tremendous transformation.

EDUCATION

Previously education was very uncommon to the people of Ranikhet. It was only after the British came here that education became popular among the masses. In the beginning there were only 5 schools in Ranikhet, namely:

1. Cantonment Primary School Sadar Bazar, Ranikhet.
2. Cantonment Primary School - Chaubattia.
3. Primary School - Kumpur.
4. Mission School, Ranikhet.
5. Government Girls Middle School, Ranikhet.

Later on, 2 more schools cropped up -

1. Urdu Medium Islamia School.
2. National School.

Later by turn of century, when you look at Ranikhet, you would see that there were as many as 80 Schools.

Besides, one Post Graduate College run by the U.P. Government, One Higher Secondary School was run by the Kendriya Vidyalaya Sangathan.

There was also one Government Inter College run by the U.P. Government. 2 Inter Colleges, 2 Middle Schools, 3 Primary Schools and 3 Montessory Schools were all run by the State Interim Zilla Parishad. Apart from these private bodies, there was an army school too.

There was also a school run by the Canossian Society of Nuns known as the Canossa Convent. Later, a public school was opened in the memory of late Seth Ghanshyamdas Birla.

PUBLIC LIBRARY

There was a Cantonment library, under the control of the Cantonment board, Sadar bazar. A public library was maintained for the benefit of public including the students, where a number of Magazines, Newspapers and Books were readily available. The library was situated near the Roadways Bus Station.

FIRE FIGHTING SERVICES

The U.P. Government had established a Fire Fighting station in Ranikhet for fire fighting purposes, in 1983, after a big fire had caught the city. Its service was very prompt and effective.

GENERAL SANITATION OF THE CANTONMENT

The general state of hygiene and sanitation of Ranikhet was satisfactory. Phenoel, Nuvan and Malarial oil were used in public ablutions (toilets/urinals) and drains as measures to avoid mosquito breeding.

Prior to 1958 there were dry type of toilets in Ranikhet and C.G.I. group toilets in the Cantonment. After the implementation of the 5 year plans, the Cantonment Board converted 18 group toilets into septic tanks. The ones, beside the residences were also persuading to provide flush type of toilets in their houses. The Cantonment Board had also provided flush type of urinals at certain places in civil areas of the Cantonment Board.

Previously, rubbish in the Cantonment was being disposed off by the buffalo carts. The removal of rubbish was creating insanitary conditions rather than the proper disposal.

During the year 1961 the Cantonment Board purchased two tempo 3 wheeler vehicles for the removal of rubbish and then the system of removal of rubbish by buffalo carts was replaced by the three wheeler tempo.

Thereafter, one Jeep entailor was purchased for the purpose. By 1990 there were 3 vehicles for the removal of rubbish and the system of removal was modern and quite satisfactory.

There were two vegetable markets. Both of them were in the Sadar Bazar.

There were two meat markets, one Jhatka and the other Halal catering to the requirements of various sects of the society. There was also a fish stall in Ranikhet.

Ranikhet is known as the "Queen of Kumaon Hills". It

was a very popular hill resort with an excellent climate. The following measures had been made by the Cantonment for the beautification of this Queen town.

Wooden umbrellas had been provided in several places for shelter and shade. There were road side gardens, and flower hanging baskets had been provided in the main localities in order to improve the scenic beauty of this panoramic Hill Station.

PLAY GROUNDS

There was no public playground in the Cantonment prior to 1954 except one playground owned by the Mission School in Rajpura.

During the year 1953-54 the residents of Ranikhet represented to the Government that the land for a playground be allotted for organizing tournaments as well as games for the students of local educational institutions. The Government very kindly acceded to the demand of the public and allotted an area of about 5 acres to the local Cantonment Board for this purpose.

The said playground was situated at a distance of nearly 2 Kms. from Ranikhet. The field was being used by the students for games as well as for organizing tournaments and was adequate to meet the requirements of the time.

The desirability of the construction of a stadium in this playground was considered very necessary, which would also suit the purpose if things materialise. Suggestively this project could be taken up by the self-help of the people of Ranikhet coupled with the resources of Government subsidies.

ELECTRIFICATION

By turn of century Ranikhet town was wholly electrified i.e. in 100% areas. The load utilization was one and half K.V. and 1500 K.Watts. Street lighting in Ranikhet was done by the Cantonment Board by way of taking energy from M.E.S. as well *as* the Hydel Department. Prior to 1954, there was no electricity in Ranikhet. During the year 1956-57 the Hydel Department installed some poles in the Sadar Bazar. During the year 1962-63 the Cantonment Board electrified the main roads and the localities in the Cantonment.

MEDICAL FACILITIES

Medical facilities provided by the means of Hospitals were thus :

1. Military Hospital, Cantonment Board, Tel. 2357/ 2358.
2. Civil Hospital near Roadways Bus Station. Tel. 2422,
3. Sitapur Eye Hospital, Shiv Mandir Marg.
4. Dr. Bangari's Clinic near Bus Station. Tel. 2345.
5. Dr. Bisht's Clinic and Drug House, Sadar Bazar. Tel. 2353.
6. Dr. U.C. Pandey's Clinic, Zaroori Bazar. Tel. 2254.

The Cantonment Board maintained of a Dispensary of its own for the benefit of the masses. The Civil Hospital was run by the U.P. Government, where all the facilities of both the outdoor and indoor treatment were available. There were two private wards in the Hospital. The total number of beds was about 100.

The State Government had allocated funds for the

expansion of the hospital. The construction of the buildings within the hospital had nearly been completed. There was an effective increase of beds after the implementation of the scheme. Treatment was also given to the adjoining villages.

A small Maternity and Child Welfare Centre was maintained by the Cantonment Board in the Cantonment Dispensary. A vaccinator was employed by the Cantonment Board for performing vaccinations.

The Eye Hospital in the Civil area of the Cantonment was hosted in its own building. Here all the facilities were given to people having eye problems.

CHEMISTS

The following Chemist shops were available in Ranikhet:

1. Kumaon Drug House and Kumaon Medical Stores, Sadar Bazar.
2. Dr. Bangari's Drug Store, Sadar Bazar.
3. Goyal Medical Store, Sadar Bazar.
4. Raj Drugs and Pharmaceuticals, Sadar Bazar.
5. Hari Ganga Medical Store, Sadar Bazar.
6. Ranikhet Drug House, Sadar Bazar.
7. Hari Har Drug Store.

These Chemists gave sufficient medical facilities to the poeple of Ranikhet.

7

Development of Transport and Communication

With the opening of Ruhelkhand Kumaon railways and the establishment of Kathgodown and Ramnagar as rail routes, the remoteness of Ranikhet was reduced to a great extent. The Rail line of Kathgodown was laid in the year 1886. Alongwith the motor road come an era of modernising influence. Buses started plying between Kathgodown and Ranikhet which were initially run by private individuals but later on 'Kumaon Motor Owners Union Limited' took up this responsibility. The first bus station was located behind what was known as the "Meghdoot Hotel". Subsequently, it shifted near the Sadar Bazar (near the present Nainital Bank) and finally landed up at its present location. After independance, the transportation system of Ranikhet had come in a big way with the Uttar Pradesh Roadways taking the major responsibility. In addition to it there were also a number of Taxi Cabs, Tourists Taxis and Private Buses available for the locals as well as tourists transportation.

AIR

The nearest Airport was at Panthnagar 119 KMs away from Ranikhet. The "Vayudoot Air Service" was available from Dehli to Panthnagar. It was a tri weekly Air Service. The mode of transport were the small Aeroplanes carrying 18 passengers at a stretch, known as the Dornier Aircraft.

RAIL

The nearest railway stations was at Kathgodown 83 KM and Ramnagar 96 KMs from Ranikhet. The Kathgodown railway line was of metre gauge where as the Ramnagar railway line was of broad guage.

ROAD

There was a net work of good road routes connecting Ranikhet. The UPSRTC (Uttar Pradesh State Road Transport Corporation) and the KMOU Ltd operated buses to different places from Ranikhet. With the passage of time the roads had all been broadened and double tracked as a means of tourists attraction.

LOCAL TRANSPORT

The local transports which were available in Ranikhet were the private taxies and the City Bus Service. Apart from it there were the "Parvat (Hill) Tours", which also catered the requirements of tourists and visitors.

8

Recreations

Pleasure seeking as they were, the Britishers enjoyed themselves in bars, clubs, motels etc. The major recreation centres were the Ranikhet Club (began by Col. Harwell), Mrs. Clarke's motel, the new Billiards Saloon and Coffee Shops, and to top it all, the sprawling Nine Hole Golf Course. However, these recreation centres were no more in existence later, except the Golf Link and the Ranikhet Club, a major portion of which was gutted in a devastating fire that broke out in August, 1987.

One of the recreations which the people of Ranikhet enjoyed was to witness the Ceremonial Parades and functions organised by the Kumaon Regimental Centre in the Centre's Parade Ground. The Raising Day was one of the auspicious occasion which a man of Ranikhet thoroughly enjoyed.

9

Development of Tourism

On the whole development in the field of tourism in Ranikhet was decreasing for last some years. Main causes were the water scarcity, lack of tourists entertainment and also lack of good accommodation. The whole anagement was under military, thus tourism also depended on the goodwill of defence. Mainly there were two sources of income for the development of tourism - Toll Barriers and Hotels. In 1986 - 2,64,781 lacs rupees were earned by toll barrier and about 28,769 lac rupees by hotels.

In 1987 - 3,40,673 rupees were earned by toll barriers and about 34,559 rupees by the hotels.

In 1988 - 3,29,410 rupees were earned by toll barriers and 38,746 rupees by hotels.

Accommodation - Situation by Nineties

1. There were about 150 beds in the tourist bungalows and 252 beds in the Mallroad.
2. Other accommodation were like this:

   i) Forest Rest House - under Residential

Authority, Kumaon Nainital.

ii) Forest Rest House, Kalika: Residential Authority DFO West Division, Almora.

3. PWD Inspection House: Residential Authority, Executive Engineer Provincial Division, PWD Ranikhet and SDM Ranikhet.
4. Ranikhet Club: Residential Authority, Secretary Ranikhet Club, Ranikhet.
5. Tourist Rest House, Mall Road: Residential Authority, Incharge Tourist Rest House, Mall Road, Ranikhet.

DHARAMSHALA

There was a Dharamshala in town, known as the Shiv Mandir Dharamshala, situated on the Shiv Mandir Marg in Zaroori Bazar - Ranikhet.

RESTAURANTS

There were a number of Restaurants both big and small in Ranikhet; catering for the requirements of the people in town. Special care was almost taken by all the Restaurant Owners to entertain the tourists. The notable Restaurants were as follows:-

1. Alka Restaurant
2. Everest Restaurant
3. Garden Cafetaria - Chaubattia.
4. Moon Restaurant
5. Mayur Restaurant.
6. Meghdoot Restaurant.

7. Sun and Snow - Kalika.
8. Seagull Restaurant.
9. Milan Restaurant.

HOTELS

Keeping in view the overflow of tourists in Ranikhet, the Hotel business was flourished to quite an extent. Although at times, the scarcity of hotels was witnessed during the peak of the season but somehow or the other tourists were always adjusted here or there although unpleasantly. The Government on the other hand was giving opportunities also to promote this business, but the response had been very poor. Truly speaking, the domination in this trade was of the SHAHS who owned both land and buildings in Ranikhet. Obviously new enterpreneurs were very suspicious about their progress, hence hesitatd to adopt this trade.

As a matter of information the following were the prominent hotels in the Ranikhet township:-

1. West View Hotel.
2. Nortons Hotel - Mall Road.
3. Meghdoot Hotel.
4. Moon Hotel.
5. Alka Hotel.
6. Hotel Tribhuwan.
7. Natraj Hotel.
8. Everest Hotel.
9. Tourists Hotel.
10. Ashok Hotel.
11. Kailash Hotel.
12. Snow View Hotel

INFORMATION CENTRE

The following were the places where one could gether all the reliable informations pertaining to the Ranikhet township and its surrounding suberbs:- (Along with their phone number by 1990)

1. UP Tourist Bureau, Near Bus Station Ranikhet, PN-2227.
2. Central Government Information Centre, Mall Road, Ranikhet.

BANKS

The following were the Banks operating in the town. The services of these banks were both trustworthy and appreciable:-

1. State Bank of India, Phone No. 2267.
2. M/s Durga Sah Mohan Lal Sah Bankers, Phone No. 2403.
3. Nainital Bank - Phone No. 2264. ;.
4. Punjab National Bank - Phone No. 2374.
5. District Cooperation Bank - Phone No. 2321.
6. Zila Gramin Bank - Chaubattia.

POST OFFICE

Speaking about the post offices of Ranikhet one must be aware that the post offices of Ranikhet at one time commanded a supremacy during the British Regime. Its promptness and reliable service was remembered even later.

The post office of the Mall Road enjoyed itself the privilege to be called a GPO. The three post offices in Ranikhet area:-

1. GPO - Mall Road.
2. Sadar Bazar Post Office.
3. Kucheri Post Office.

SHOPPING CENTRES

Unlike the shopping Arcades of prominent hill stations of Simla and Srinagar the Shopping Centres of Ranikhet had a very traditional outlook.

One would not find a very posh shop, but the requirements of locals as well as tourists were fulfilled by these shops very successfully.

In fact, there were four Shopping Centres (Bazars) namely the Sadar Bazar, Khari Bazar, Zaroori Bazar and the Bazar in the Mall Road. Not very scattered, all the four Bazars were situated near by. Later developments showed that new shops had come up as a means of progress which was certainly a further step towards the renovation of town and the marketing area.

The tourist attractions were the shops selling the natural wood crafts. Neatly decorated and painted wooden materials procured from the forest (chir forest) were kept for sale, as "decoration pieces", which were sold like hot cakes, because of its uniqueness and antiquity.

PLACES OF RELIGIOUS IMPORTANCE

The places of Religious importance were very many but naming the few which were a centre of attraction were as follows:-

1. Shiv Mandir - Zaroori Bazar.
2. Mankameshwar Temple - near Nar Singh Ground.
3. Sri Ram Mandir - Hanuman Temple and Jhula Devi.
4. Harakhan Temple Chillianaula.
5. Kali Temple - Kalika.
6. Gurdawara Near Nar Singh Ground.
7. Jamia Masjid.
8. Catholic Church - Upper Mall.
9. English Methodist Church - Upper Mall.
10. St. Martin's Church.
11. Balmiki Temple with Dharamshala.

Visiting the various temples one could see the old as well as the new temples built in Ranikhet. Both had their esteem values in common but with a different architectural design. One would notice a fair combination of the ancient and the modern. The Hedakhan temple of Chillianaula was a remarkable piece of modern architecture whereas the Shiv Mandir of the Zaroori Bazar was an ancient design par-excellence.

CLUBS

The two Clubs which were both famous and prominent are:-

1. The Ranikhet Club.
2. The Rotary Club.

CINEMAS

There were three Cinema Halls in Ranikhet: They were:-

1. Globe Theatre

2. Ratan Palace
3. Lecture Theatre

MAJOR FESTIVALS OF RANIKHET

In Ranikhet culture was still flourishing in its original form. On seeing the people following their customs and traditions without any restriction one was certainly delighted.

Tracing the history one will come to know that from the very beginning the following three functions (Festivals) were very predominently celeberated. They were the Shiv Ratri, the Krishna Janmashtami and the Nanda Devi.

Speaking truly the people of Ranikhet appeared to be quite religiously indoctrinated. Looking at the mammoth gathering of persons during the Festive Occasions, it leaves no doubt to judge the cultural awareness of the people, coupled with their consciousness of religion.

AUTOMOBILES

The automobiles which were famous in Ranikhet were the following :

1. Latif Motor Works - Sadar Bazar
2. Rudri Workshop - Shamim Automobiles.

Apart from it, skilled automobile technicians were also in town who took up private contract jobs of both two wheelers and four wheelers.

10

Places of Tourist Importance

CHAUBATTIA

10 Kms from Ranikhet, was a garden spot commanding a fascinating view of the Himalayas. The chief attractions of the place were Government Garden and the Fruit Research Centre attached to it. Varities of Apples were available for sale at Chaubattia during the fruit season.

Brief History & Achievements of Horticultural Experiments & Training Centre - Chaubattia:

Temperate fruit cultivation in the hills of UP started with the advent of British Officers and retired settlers from other countries of those who were familiar with temperate fruit orchards in the foreign countries.

The success achieved by some of the enterprising Europeans in temperate fruit cultivation in Kumaon attracted the attention of the State Government as early as 1869, and a Government orchard was started at Chaubattia to ensure

free distribution of the temperate fruit plants suitable for the climate and soil of the Himalayan region. A *large* number of fruit trees were distributed but unfortunately majority of these trees could not come to the majority due to inexperience and lack of proper guidance. Various problems started cropping up e.g. heavy rains followed by long spell of dry period. The diversity in soil conditions with varying terrain and altitudes often proved fatal to the new orchards. In order to solve the enormous problems faced by the orchardists, the hill fruit Research Station, Chaubattia was established in the year 1932.

This is the oldest Research Station on temperate fruit in India. It has done excellent work in improving temperate fruit cultivation in the UP hills as well as in the other temperate regions of the country.

Due to the adoption of improved cultural methods evolved at Chaubattia, the yield had risen considerably, which was significant of an experienced research work and technical expertise.

The results of practical importance achieved at the Research Station were being carried to the cultivators for application on field scale through the extension service staff of the Directorate. The cultivators were also given advise in selecting the sites, laying out of orchards, digging, manuring, soil conservation, pruning and over and above how to control the diseases on the horticultural crops.

Numerous specimens consisting of soil samples fungus or insects infested plants, fruits and vegetables were received regularly at the station for its identification and analytical study as a part of the horticultural development programme.

After necessary investigation prompt advise was given to the cultivators on the subject. About 400 publications comprising of technical papers, bulletins and leaflets etc had been published by the Research Station in Hindi and English for the use of cultivation and extension of workers.

The Research Station was also the Training Centre for the extension workers i.e. Development Officers, Gram Sewak, Extension Teachers mails etc. The trainees from Nepal, Afghanistan, Sikkim, Bhuttan, Manipur etc have also been trained at Chaubattia, Ranikhet.

The Station was a recognised centre for conducting research work leading to Ph.D degree in all plan disciplines.

The research work carried out in the station had been divided into 9 sections viz:

1. Vegetables.
2. horticulture.
3. Fruit and Vegetable Breeding.
4. Soil Chemistry.
5. Plant Physiology.
6. Mycology.
7. Entomology.
8. Virus and Mushroom.
9. Drugs.

The Hill Fruit Research Station, Chaubattia was situated near Ranikhet proper. The annual rainfall was about 50 inches and the temperature varies from 23°F in winter to 90°F in summer.

The area of orchard was near by 158.61 acres of which about 100 acres are under cultivation. The remaining portion was under the forest belt.

Orchard was started in 1869-70 by the Forest Department but was handed over to the Agricultural Department in 1914. The innumerable big orchards that have

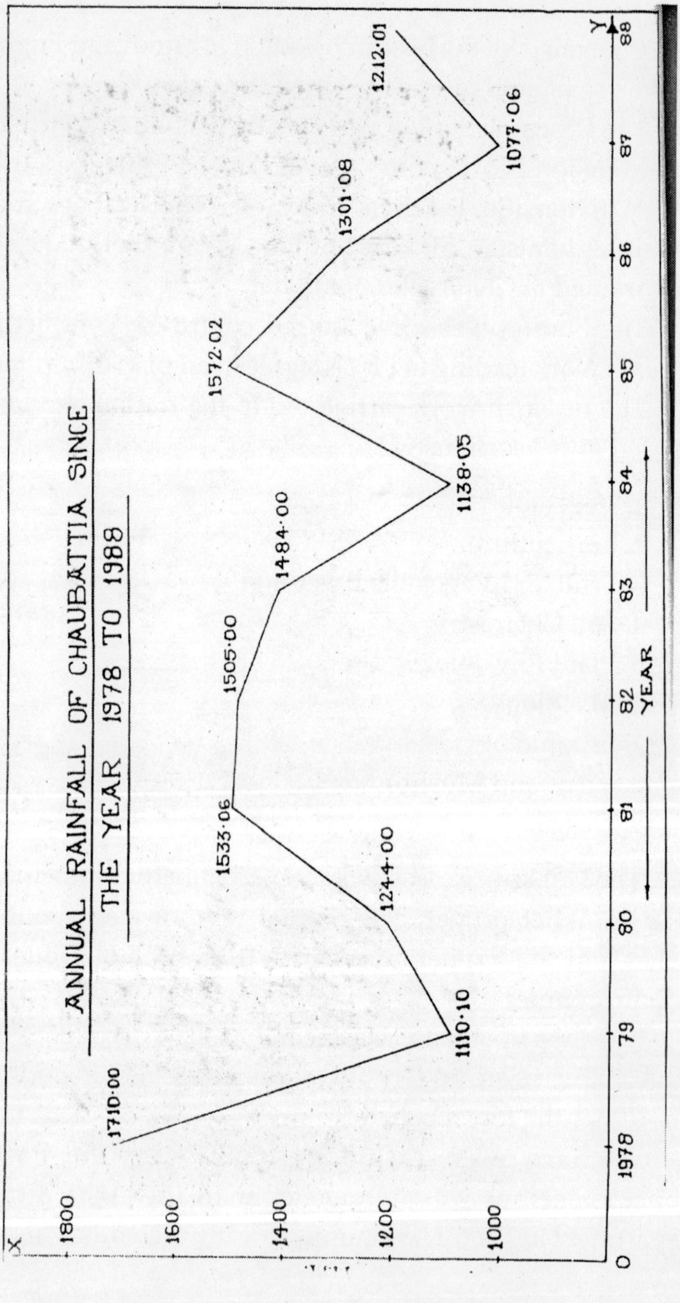
ANNUAL RAINFALL OF CHAUBATTIA SINCE
THE YEAR 1978 TO 1988
X
1800
1600
1400
1200
1000
0
Y
1978
79
80
81
82
83
84
85
86
87
88
YEAR
1710·00
1110·10
1244·00
1533·06
1505·00
1484·00
1138·05
1572·02
1301·08
1077·06
1212·01

sprung up in Kumaon owe their origin in some way or the other to this orchard.

Area of Chaubattia Orchard was 135 acres. Fruit and Vegetable Breeding was started at this station since 1970.

Work in Plant Physiology Section was started from 1902 on the Chemical analysis of various hill fruits.

Every year training on Mushroom cultivation was being imparted at both the stations according to the target allotted by the Government since 1972.

Here was also a great scope for cultivation of medical plants. This centre had many sub-stations under its technical guidance. There were two high altitudes research stations where research work was concentrated on temperate nuts and two valley fruit research stations.

The orchard had an elevation of 6,100 to 6,700 Ft above the sea level. Soil was mostly clayey but had considerable variation.

Fruit Production in Chaubattia Garden in the Year 1987-88

1. Apples	13,800 M.T
2. Pear	1,875 M.T.
3. Peaches	2,280 M.T.
4. Citrus	1,100 M.T.
5. Plum and Apricot	3,255 M.T.
6. Walnuts	500 M.T.
7. Others	187 M.T.

Vegetable Production In The Year 1987-88

1. Potato 2,468 M.T.
2. Others 9,516 M.T.

Total Export of Fruits From Chaubattia Garden in 1987-88 692 Qntl.

These figures can easily show the production and profit gained by the orchard.

KALIKA and UPAT

6 Kms from the bus station along the main road of Almora, Upat was one of the best mountain links (9 holes) in the country, while at near by, the Kalika, the temple of Goddess Kali and the Forest Nursery was worth visiting.

The Forest department of UP had a research nursery at this place. This nursery had tried 70 species of pine and 38 that of Eucalyptus. Out of which 40 species of pine and 24 species of Eucalyptus was growing successfully.

Particularly, this Kalika nursery alone could make students aware of about thousand species of plants which a botanist could see only by visiting the whole of Himalaya from Kashmir to Assam.

Kalika put forth some remarkable collection of species of Pine, Eucalyptus, Acacia and Cypresses selected from through out the world. The Kalika nursery claims to have one of the rare and ancient tree termed by the botanists "as the living fossil", which dates back to the carbon Age of 60 lakh years of age.

BHALUDAM

This small artificial lake was at a little less than 3 Kms distance from Chaubattia by the Briddle Road.

CO-OPERATIVE DRUGS FACTORY

The factory was engaged in the research work and production of Ayurvedic drugs from local medicinal herbs. It was about 3 Kms from the bus stand on the road to Ramnagar.

CHILLIANAULA

About 4 Kms from Ranikhet Chillianula was famous for the temple of Baba Hedakhan. It commanded a Panaramic view of the extensive Himalayas. The Saraswati Woolen Mills and the GD Birla Memorial School was also there. A Post Graduate College was also situated in Chillianaula.

JHULADEVI

Situated at a distance of 7 Kms from Ranikhet on the way to Chaubattia gardens. Jhuladevi was famous for the temple of Goddess Durga and Sri Ram Mandir. People had an undaunted faith in this temple, hence worshippers came here in large numbers to get their dreams fulfilled.

TARIKHET

A developing township, Tarikhet was 8 Kms from Ranikhet on the Motor Road to Ramnagar. Mahatma Gandhi had visited and stayed at Tarikhet for some time. A kuti (hut appartment) commemorated his visit to the spot.

An ancient temple of God "Gwela" was also there.

MAJKHALI

A picturesque spot at a distance of 13 Kms from Ranikhet on the motor road to Almora, Majkhali offerd a close view of the snowy heights.

DWARAHAT

It had once been the principal seat of the Katyuri Rajas. It had a cluster of age old temples, divided into 8 distinct groups.

DUNAGIRI

It was a place of religious importance. It was famous for its temple of the Goddess Durga "Vaishnavi" which had an inscription dating back to 1181 AD. One could have a good view of Gagas and Someshwar-Almora Valleys both and a view of Almora Town.

SITALAKHET

The view of the snows from Sitalakhet was ideal for a peaceful holiday here. It obtained a beautiful birds eye view of the town of Almora.

MANILA

Manila was the charming back drop of the snow clad mountains.

KHAIRNA

Khairna was famous for fishing. It had once been the life line of the Kumaon region.

11

Ranikhet—The Centre of Kumaon Regiment

In the lap of the snow capped Himalayas between the Kingdom of Nepal and the Indian district of Garhwal lies Kumaon, also known as Kurmanchal.

The home of the Kumaonees and the so called Kumaon regiment did not always have its home among the lush hills of Kumaon. Moreso it was not known by its name till recent years. Some of the battalions have a history that goes to the closing decades of the 18th century. Retracing that history we find that the Kumaon regiment was born far away in the Deccan where some of its units were raised as a part of the Nizam of Hyderabad whose descendents ruled that state, till recently.

It was in the year 1780 that the 2nd Battalion (BERAR) now 2 Kumaon was originally raised at Hyderabad in the services of the earstwhile Hyderabad state. This was closely followed by Salabat Khan regiment in 1788 (now a Kumaon) at Ellichpur by Nawab Salabat Khan. The designation of the regiment underwent numerous changes from time to time.

Later, Sir Henry Russel the then resident of the earstwhile Hyderabad state laid the real foundation of the regiment when two battalions as first and second battalion were raised, Russel brigade was raised in 1813. They were redesignated as Hyderabad contingent in 1854. The advent of World War 1st added the 4/39th the Garhwal Rifles later renamed 4/39th Kumaon Rifles and now 3 Kumaon Rifles.

The battalion was raised in Ranikhet in 1917 during World War 1st and IInd. The regiment distinguished itself on active service in various overseas theatres of war in Mesopatamia, China, East Africa, Turkey, Egypt, Palestine, Malaya, Burma and particularly excellent in the battle of Sharan (Palestine) in the 1918 and Kangaw (Burma) in 1945 inflicting heavy casualities on Turkish and Japanese forces respectively. During World War IInd six more battalions were raised to meet the heavy demand. These were 5, 7, 8, 9, 25th and 26th battalions. It was in the year 1922, on regrouping of the Indian army, the requirement was redesignated as 19th Hyderabad regiment the 6/19th Hyderabad Regiment. It was now the 6th battalion the Kumaon Regiment in 1941. On 27th October 1945 the regiment assumed its present designation as the Kumaon Regiment.

In the post independent invasions of Kashmir by Pakistan, the Kumaon regiment was instrumental in meeting the challenge of large scale, infiltration across the border.

Infact Major Somnath Sharma's 4 Kumaon averted a national disorder by not allowing the enemy to capture Srinagar airfield at Badgaun. Though the brave and heroic Officer lost his life, he earned the regiment's 1st Param Vir Chakra awarded to an Indian soldier. In 1949 Maj. General K. S. Thimayya D.S.C. was appointed as the first Indian Colonel of this regiment.

In 1959 the Kumaon went to serve in the United Nations Peace Keeping

Force in Gaza. It returned in 1960 and in 1961 became the first Unit in independent India to receive the President's colour in a magnificient and impressive ceremony at Ranikhet.

In 1962, during the Sino-Indian conflict at walling NEFA and Regangla (Ladakh) Kumaoni battalion fought courageous and tenacious battles to the finish. Sacrifice and devotion to duty for the defence of the motherland became synonymous with the Kumaon Regiment.

In Regangla almost all ranks sacrificed their lives to save Chushul and in turn Ladakh itself. It was here that the courageous, inspiring, devoted and heroic Major Shaitan Singh (13 Kumaon) nobly laid down his life in the battle. He was awarded the Param Vir Chakra for his exemplary leadership in the battle.

Again in 1965, when Pakistan attacked India, the regiment added a golden chapter to the record of its already glittering achievement and won many covetted awards.

On 27th October, 1970 the regiment received colours at Ranikhet from Shri V.V. Giri the then President of India. In 1970, the same year the Naga regiment (Now 1 Naga) was raised at Ranikhet and was affiliated to the Kumaon regiment.

In May 1971, late General T.N.Raina M.V.C. took over as Colonel of the regiment from Lt. General K. Bahadur Singh. In December, 1971 when Pakistan invaded India, yet again, the Kumaon, and the Naga regiment were crucial in defeating the Pakistan army and helping Bangladesh to attain the freedom.

In January, 1978, 18 Kumaon was raised. On 6th May

General T.N. Raina M.V.C. then C.O.A.S. and Colonel of the regiment presented them with regimental colours. The Naga regiment was presented colours by Shri Neelam Sanjeevi Reddy, the then President of India. One day later i.e. on 7th May, 1978, the 19th Kumaon regiment, the 20th Kumaon regiment and Kumaon Scouts battalions were presented colours. In 1984 the then COAS Lt. Gen P.N. Kathpalia A.V.S.M. took over as the colonel of the regiment from A.S. Vaidya, P.V.S.M., M.V.C. and who worked in this capacity till 3rd October, 1985. On 4th October, 1985 Lt. General R.N. Mahajan V.S.M. took over as the colonel of the regiment from him.

HOME OF KUMAON REGIMENT; RANIKHET

The Kumaon Regimental Centre was the mother institution of the Kumaon regiment. It was here that we transform a raw Kumaoni boy coming from the remote corner of Kumaon hills into an energetic and budding soldier of the regiment. They had the best of Instructors there, who took ardous pain to train the recruits on completion of 36 weeks of basic training. These recruits were attested and sent to various active battlions of the regiment. It was here that a Kumaoni soldier learn the rudimentary lessons of soldiering. It was here that he fires the first shot from his basic weapon on a paper target. Gradually his confidence was enhanced by firing on the similar targets at varying distances to achieve the aim of the soldier to shoot to kill (enemy). *

The centre did not confine its activities to recruit's training only. It had many other responsibilities to perform. Being the home of the regiment its major resources were diverted towards the welfare of our troops. As mother institute, it had the onus responsibility of preserving the cultural and historical heritage of the regiment. It had also the responsibility of preserving the sanctity of those brave Kumaonees who had laid down their lives while defending the long drawn border of the country. To this end they had instituted various projects and memorials in the centre, Ranikhet.

The welfare projects were designed to help rehabilitate those who had lost their near and dear ones while defending the sanctity and integrity of our great country. This was also to benefit serving the ex-servicemen of the regiment for their rehabilitation. Memorials were for those who had sacrificed their Today for our Tomorrow. Some of these projects and memorials are discussed briefly.

WAR MEMORIALS

This is located on the road side of Ranikhet Almora road in the area of Dulikhet Training Ground Complex. The idea of the construction of this War Memorial was conceived by the then Colonel of the regiment late Gen. T.N. Raina, M.V.C. in 1972. The foundation stone was laid on 8th April, 1974 by late Colonel P.C. Mehta, A.V.S.M. the then Commandant of the centre. The need was felt to remind the present and the future generations. The supreme sacrifices made by the martyrs while defending the sanctity of the borders of our motherland in various wars fought since independence including counter insurgency operations in the North Eastern States of the Nagaland and Mizoram and also while encountering the terrorists, like the Operation Blue Star in Punjab. The layout of the War Memorial was designed by late Miss Shona Ray an eminent architect and art designer of Delhi.

The design of the War Memorial depicts the field of "Mother's Lap" on I I which, each of us, develop the strength to grow and is finally put to sleep for ever.

The Mother's Lap is made out of Golden coloured Jaisalmere stone on which the names of the brave sons of the regiment are etched. The memorial was inaugerated by late General T. N. Raina, M.V.C. with full military honours on 14th October, 1974.

The recruits of Kumaon and Naga regiment both on reporting at the centre while Zero Week and again after attestation, paid homage to the sacred memorial to draw inspiration from the valiant deeds of the brave martyrs of the regiment and pledge to uphold the highest tradition of the Kumaon and Naga Regiments. Special War Memorial services were also conducted when the V.I.P.s visited the station.

Of late, they had started the War Memorial services every day between 0730 hrs. to 0830 hrs. in the War Memorial, for witnessing by our civilians of Ranikhet. They had to see, many of our civilians attending this sacred service for those who had sacrificed their lives at the lltar of their duty.

MUSEUM

The idea of having a museum at the Centre was conceived by late (General T.N. Raina, M.V.C. when he was performing the duty of Colonel of the regiment. One of the responsibilities that had been bestowed upon [the Centre, Ranikhet, was to preserve the cultural heritage of our regiment and troops. This amounts to compiling day to day events of the historical values of the regiments. These were then reproduced in the form of the regiment's history. To highlighten the history of this 'regiment, this museum had been established. The basic theme of this was to depict the important events wherein the regiment had assailed so far, ever since its inception.

The foundation stone of the museum was laid on 29th October, 1976 by the late General T.N. Raina. M.V.C. It was inaugurated by him on 20th May, 1978. The museum had been designed and constructed by a well known designer and architect.

It has 5 cubes with pyramid shaped roof which symbolizes the shape of a Temple, Church, Gompa, Masjid and Gurudwara, thus signifying unity and j true secularism. The layout of the panels, brigades and various display articles had been done by the famous interior decorator Mrs. Rosemary Sachdev. The total cost incurred for construction was 19 lacs. Visitors get complete historical background of the regiment in a chronological order. They hope to allow more of the civilians to visit the museum so that they also come to know the regiment's history with the passage of time.

REHABILITATION

Our troops retire at an early age. The majority of troops go on pension when their children are still on the verge of completion of their education. To cater for their requirement the regiment had undertaken the responsibility of providing facilities to the servicemen or their dependents. The following disciplines of vocational trainings were being imparted:

BANDAGE. SHAWL AND TWEED MAKING;

This training has provided to the widows of the troops and their children who were desirous of undertaking this, projected to them. They (the widows and children of troops) were paid a stipend of Rs. 100/- per month.

CARPENTRY

Many people attended this course. Keeping in view the forest belt around and the necessity to impart training in wood work, stress was given to the carpentry training as a means of immediate livelihood.

GENERAL MECHANIC COURSE

This included welding, leather and electrical works. Development in this field had been gradual, but efforts were being taken by many a people to start their own small scale industry after undertaking the course The Government was also providing necessary assistance to interested persons in this line through their District Industrial Centres.

SARAI

The Sarai was constructed at a cost of Rs. 2,21,083 from U.P. post war reconstruction funds. The foundation stone of this Sarai was laid by General P.N. Kathpalia. A.V.S.M. The main aim of the Sarai was to provide accomodation to servicemen, Ex-Servicemen and their dependents when they visited Ranikhet. Boarding facilities were provided on a very nominal charge of Rs. 3/- per day.

WAR MEMORIAL HOSTEL

The War Memorial Hostel had been made to benefit the school going children of the servicemen and Ex-servicemen. The charges were worked out on the basis of the pay scale. Extra expenditure incurred on the food, electricity and other miscellaneous aspects are paid by the regiment. «

COMMUNITY CENTRE

The Kumaon Regimental Centre created two community centres; one at Ranikhet and the other at Dulikhet. Some of the shops that were available at these centres are :

i. C.S.D. Canteen
ii. Wet Canteen
iii. Vegetable Shops
iv. Tailor's Shop
v. Barber's Shop
vi. Cobler's Shop
vii. Candle and Soda factory viii Mushroom Garden ix Carpentry Shop x Camera Club

By the help of this they had been able to cover the important aspects of the Regimental Centre.

12

Water Supply in Ranikhet Town

(By end of twentieth century)

Specified information in respect of the above is furnished below:-

1. Area G.E. (M.E.S.) Ranikhet under C.W.E.(P),
2. Place Ranikhet and Ranikhet Chaubattia.
3. Type of Supply : M.E.S. Pumping and Bulk Supply from U.P. Jal Nigam.

SOURCE OF WATER. SUPPLY WITH LOCATION;

i) Bhalu Dam: Water supply was from natural water springs No. 1 and 2 at Upper side of the Bhalu Dam, which was at a distance of 3.5 Kms. from Nagpani and the highest point.
ii) Kaligadhera: This Dam was at a distance of 1 Km from the Somnath ground at Ranikhet.
iii) Bulk supply of water was done from U.P. Jal Nigam at Jhuladevi water supply installations.
iv) Reoni Dam was at a distance of 12 Kms. from Ranikhet.

The area North East of the main Ranikhet Chaubattia ridge was well I rained throughout by a number of streams flowing in the general. Northerly and north easterly direction. The streams flowed from the Ranikhet Bazar station area, from compartments 1,2,3,4,5 and 50 towards the Gagas and Ramganga river system. The streams in the remaining ompartments North East of the main ridge and North West of Chaubattia, drained towards Kaligadhera and thence to the Kosi.

The streams in the compartment East of Chaubattia and North of main ridge drain towards the Sirot river which also joined the Kaligadhera.

The drainage from the compartments situated on the South West slope of the main Ranikhet Chaubattia ridge was towards the Kuch Gadhera, which met the Kosi just above Khairna.

Water supply was maintained by pumping and filtering the station at lagpani in Kuch Gadhera water walls and augmented by the Cantonment Board water supply from mint and X-Springs.

Water was taken in bulk from M.E.S. for supplying the same to the civilian inhabitants of Ranikhet. Water scarcity in the station was felt during summer months due to the huge influx of tourists. The desirability of taking resources to suppliment the water supply was being explored by the M.E.S. and Cantonment Board too. Besides, water was supplied by Gagas river direct to M.E,S. to extend the capacity.

Water at the rate of 6.76 per thousand gallon was supplied to the Cantonment Board. U.P.Jal Nigam gave water to M.E.S. and M.E.S. supplied it to the Cantonment Board. The demand of M.E.S. was near 230 lac litres of water. Proper water supply started in 1927, in Ranikhet.

13

Electric Supply and Distribution in Ranikhet

(Till last decade of century)

Electrical Sub Stations	Existing Installations
Upper Mall	150 K.W.
Lower Mall	200 K.W.
Dulikhet	50 K.W.
Ghigarikhal	35 K.W.
Jhula Devi	50 K.W.
Spring Field	100 K.W.
Chaubattia	100 K.W.
Nagpani	150 K.W
Highest Point	60 K.W.
Lift	Mil

The Distribution complex of Electricity in Ranikhet town is like this:

1. Ghingarikhal

Maximum demand	65 K.W.
Availability	35 K.W.
Deficiency	30 K.W.

Source	U.P.S.E.B.
Nature of supply	LT 3 Q, 400V, 50 CY.
Stand by Generator	Nil
Feeding Areas	Infantary battalion (13 K.R.) Officer's Mess Single Officer's Quarters Coy Line Battalion Stores Officer's Unit Line and Ranges.

2. Dulikhet

Maximum demand	Availability
50 K.W.	50 K.W.
Deficiency	Nil
Source	U.P.S.E.B.
Nature of supply	LT 3 Q, 400V, 50 CY
Standby Generator	Nil
Feeding areas	Gymnasium Officer's Bungalows ALFA COY KRC C.B. M.D. JCO's Quarters ORs Quarters Quarter Guard

3. Lower Mall

Maximum demand	250 K.W.
Availability	200 K.W.
Deficiency	50 K.W.
Source	U.P.S.E.B.
Nature of supply	LT 3 Q, 400V, 50 CY
Standby generator	Nil

Feeding areas	Kaligadhera Pumps Central School Museum Globe Cinema Lecture Hall K.R.C. HQ./Sub. HQ. Garrison Engineer's Office Key Personnel Qtrs. ASC EME MDF Cantonment Board Depot. CoY Officer's Bungalow Half Moon Lines JCO's/ORs Married Qtrs, Separated family Qtrs. Ranges ASC Butchery

4 Upper Mall

Maximum demand	200 K.W.
Availability	Deficiency
Source	150 K.W.
50 K.W.	U.P.S.E.B.
Nature of supply	LT 3 Q, 400V, 50 CY
Standby generator	15 K.W.
Feeding areas	Military Hospital MDC Officer's Bungalows Officer's Mess KRC Kumaon House & Lodge Single Officer's Quarters

	Record Office Canossa Convent School & Church Street lights Telephone Exchange & Bandage Factory

5. Nagpani

Maximum demand	150 K.W.
Availability	150 K.W.
Deficiency	Nil
Source	U.P.S.E.B.
Nature of supply	LT 3 Q, 400V, 50 CY.
Feeding area	Nagpani
Pumping Installation	Nil

6. Highest Point

Maximum demand	65 K.W.
Availability	65 K.W.
Deficiency	Nil
Source	U.P.S.E.B.
Nature of supply	LT 3 Q, 400V, 50 CY.
Standby generator	62.5 KVA
Feeding area	Pumping
Installation	Highest Point

7. Chaubattia

Maximum demand	150 K.W.
Availability	100 K.W.
Deficiency	50 K.W.
Source	U.P.S.E.B.
Nature of supply	LT 3 Q, 400V, 50 CY

Standby generator	62.5 K.W.
Feeding areas	B.D.E. HQ
Signal CoY Exchange	23 Wireless Technical Wing A.W.D. Workshop Officer's Mess Infantary Battalion (7 Garhwal) Ranges Married Accomodation for Officers JCOs/ORs Quarters
Feeding area generator set	Only essential load of 23 Wireless Technical wing.

8. Jhuladevi

Maximum demand	75 K.W.
Availability	Nil
Deficiency	75 K.W.
Source	U.P.S.E.B.
Nature of supply	LT 3 Q, 400V, 50 CY
Standby generator	Nil
Feeding areas	Jhula Devi Pumps Inspection Bungalows Gandhi Barracks/ Quarters

Other Important Information

1. Minimum Charges :
   Rs. 15/- per K.W. on 60% of the maximum demand.
2. <u>Rate of Supply as per Agreement</u>
   Upto 10,000 Units
   25 N.P.
   Next 20,000 Units
   25 N.P.
   In excess of 30,000 ... 19 N.P.

14

Miscellaneous

Forests in Ranikhet were so thick that no bungalow could be seen by the road side, although every bungalow was approachable by road.

Ranikhet had a lot of potentialities to be tapped in the private sector as high altitude floriculature nursery, horticulture nursery and herbaria collections. Ranikhet presents for a botanist three most natural open herbaria like Kalika, Chaubattia and Forest Rest House, (Mall Road).

Known personalities except Rai Sahibs were Sri Purnanand Upadhyaya (Advocate), Sri Ghananand Tiwari-Incharge KMOU Limited (the only Taxi Owner) Bhai Saheb (Advocate) Ramdutt Vaidjee and Nathuram Upreti were cultural pillars, Hargovind Pant and Madan Mohan Upadhyaya were freedom fighters the only Britisher was Col. Harwell, (the founder member of Ranikhet Club) and a bearded Pandit with his turbon mirjai and dhoti (Sri Jaidatt Joshi).

Conclusions

All said and done it is quite evident that there had been a world of difference between the Ranikhet of British days and the Ranikhet of post independence era. The sophistication, the regalia, the splendour had been supplanted by the harsh and crude realities prevailing in the Indian masses and it is quite understandable.

In an age of cut throat competition, petty rivalries, intervective :onflicts, puerile interests and obscurantist tendencies, how can a town; escape that contagious to comparative remotness? Ranikhet, is not accepted as a grand old man was commenting "Ranikhet is no longer the veritable heaven as it used to be." Yet it was undoubtedly one of the most Beautiful, civilised and cultured towns of the Kumaon region which had seen its better days and was wishfully hoping to see even better days in the future.

6. ATKINSON T.E.(1973) - The Himalayan Gazet
Vol III (1), Cosmo Publication, Delhi-2, India.
7. Baridutt Pandey-History of Kumaun 1937-Page
P- 1, 2, 3, Page 104-105
8. Contemporary documents from "Cantonr
Library" Sadar Bazar.
9. Contemporary books documents and magaz
from "Public Library". (Near Roadways Bust st

References

1. Working Plan of Ranikhet Cantonment, Uttar Pradesh.
2. A Report on Kumaon Regimental Centre.
3. Report on the working and administration of the United Provinces Government Garden for the year 1921 to 1930. Printed by :he Superintendent, Government Press, United Provinces Page 1 to 20.
4. "Sharadotsava Smarika" -1986 & 1987 Ranikhet.
5. ATKINSON T.E.(1973) - The Himalayan Gazetteer, Vol I, Page 9, Para 2, Cosmo Publication, Delhi-2, India